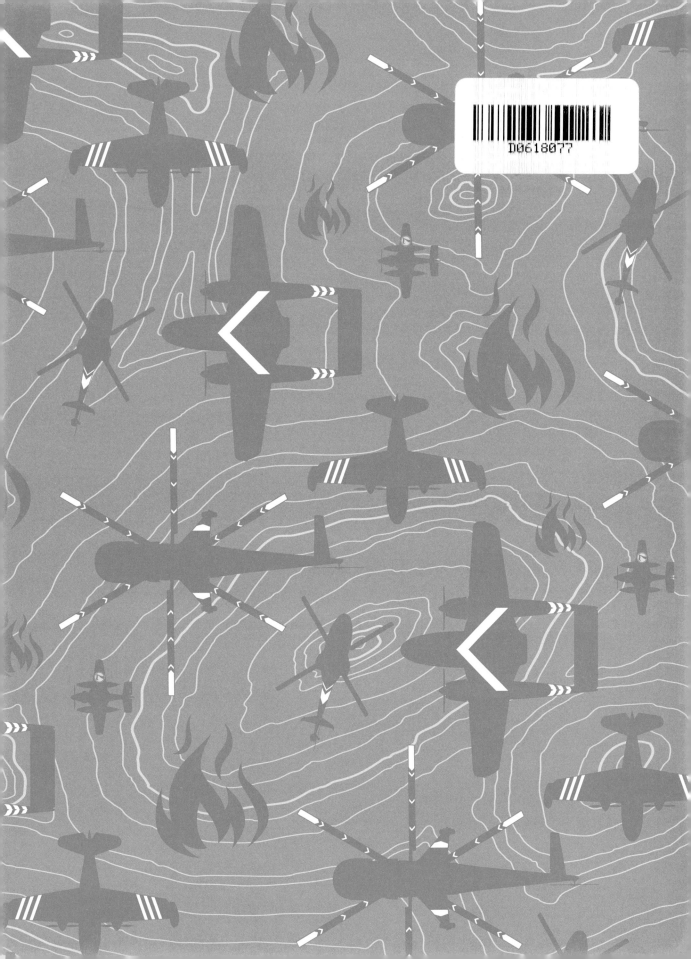

THE ESSENTIAL GUIDE

THE ESSENTIAL GUIDE

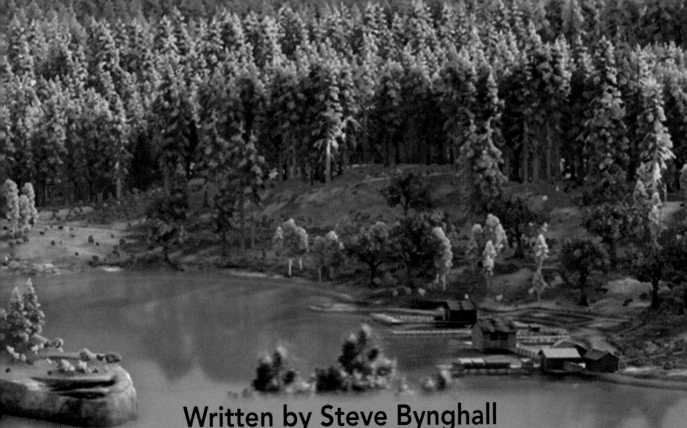

Written by Steve Bynghall

CONTENTS

INTRODUCTION

Champion racing plane Dusty Crophopper is at the peak of his career, with a hangar full of trophies and fans all over the world. However, turbulent times are ahead for Dusty.

First Dusty encounters gearbox problems. Then he accidentally starts a fire in his home town of Propwash Junction. When aging fire truck Mayday struggles to put out the flames, it is clear that the veteran firefighter needs help, as well as a whole new set of modern equipment!

The town must find a second firefighter fast to make sure visitors to the upcoming annual Corn Festival will be safe! Dusty agrees to take on his toughest challenge yet—to become a certified fire rescue plane in record speed!

Soon Dusty is training with some of the bravest rescue planes and vehicles around, the elite air attack team at Piston Peak National Park. However, with a tough teacher like veteran rescue copter Blade Ranger, ongoing gearbox problems, and threats from real fires, the heat is truly on for Dusty!

Dusty the Champ

Racing sensation Dusty Crophopper has been on an amazing journey. This agricultural plane swapped a career spraying crops for the excitement of the racing world, and ended up winning the famous Wings Around The Globe Rally! Dashing Dusty is now a racing legend with fans all over the world.

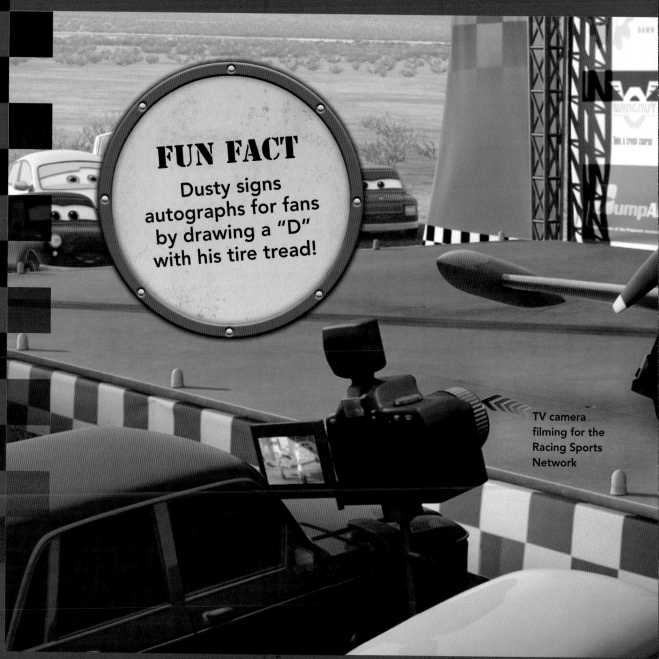

FUN FACT

Dusty signs autographs for fans by drawing a "D" with his tire tread!

TV camera filming for the Racing Sports Network

Determined Dusty

It was determination as well as talent that made Dusty a champion. He trained hard and never gave up. Dusty also overcame many hurdles, such as crashing, being scared of heights, and dealing with dirty tricks from rotten racing rival Ripslinger.

The Reno Gold trophy is Dusty's latest prize.

"I'M FEELING GOOD ABOUT MY NEXT RACE!"

Propwash Junction

Not much happens in Propwash Junction. This small, sleepy, crop-growing country town is in the middle of nowhere. Few vehicles visit and those that do mainly just pass through. But all that is about to change. Propwash Junction is soon to celebrate its Corn Festival, featuring a flying display from superstar Dusty. Crowds of visitors will be jetting in from far and wide!

① Airport
Propwash Junction's airport ensures a happy landing for all visitors. The air traffic control tower coordinates all the activity in the air, making sure everyone touches down on the runway safely.

Skipper's hangar

② Honkers Sports Bar
Honkers is where the locals hang out, sip oil, and watch sport on the TV. It even has line dancing and honky-tonk music! After a hard practice session or just to decompress, Dusty comes here to relax.

❸ Fill 'n' Fly
Chug and Dottie run the Fill 'n' Fly, the town's only service station. They take care of all their customers' vehicular needs, from topping up gas to repairing minor injuries.

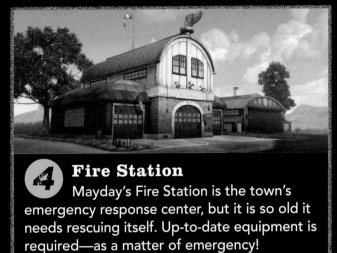

❹ Fire Station
Mayday's Fire Station is the town's emergency response center, but it is so old it needs rescuing itself. Up-to-date equipment is required—as a matter of emergency!

❹ Fire Station

Dusty's hangar

The Landing Zone

❶ Airport

❸ Fill 'n' Fly

❷ Honkers Sports Bar

Propwash Junction lies on top of a high, plane-shaped plain. Its runway goes from one edge of the plain to the other.

Old Friends

Dusty's pals from Propwash Junction are a loyal bunch. Chug, Sparky, and Dottie help to prepare, repair, and train Dusty, and when he is racing they cheer him on. Dusty may have left his old job behind, but he has not left his old friends behind. They mean more to him than winning any race.

Hook for towing vehicles »»»

Chug

Fuel truck Chug is Dusty's best and oldest buddy. The two friends still hang out and share a can of oil, just like they used to. Down-to-earth Chug keeps Dusty's wheels on the runway!

Wear and tear to bumper »»»»

TRUE OR FALSE?
Chug always repairs Dusty when his parts need fixing.

FALSE! Dottie is the pitty in charge of repairing Dusty

Team Dusty

Dusty would never have had the confidence to become a champion without the support of his buddies. In particular Chug helped him out with his hours and hours of practicing.

Missing gearbox

When Dusty's gearbox fails him, his friends do not! They try hard to find him a new one. When Dusty is away from Propwash Junction they give progress reports via the radio, but find it hard to break bad news to him this way.

Peaked >>> roof

Sparky

Sparky has an endless list of skills and a limitless supply of enthusiasm. The tireless tug never runs out of gas and always finds the energy to help his friends out.

Carries tools to tackle any job

Dottie

Mechanic Dottie is engineer-in-chief to Dusty. The plain-talking pitty skillfully repairs the champ when she can, but sometimes has to deliver bad news when she can't!

FRIENDS' TOP 3
WAYS TO SUPPORT DUSTY

🔥 Dottie – Showing patience in making dozens of repairs to Dusty

🔥 Chug – Just being there for Dusty

🔥 Sparky – Working all hours to find that elusive gearbox for Dusty

13

Skipper

Navy veteran Skipper used to train the legendary Jolly Wrenches fighter squadron, but since retiring he has become a fixture at Propwash Junction. Skipper trained Dusty to become a world-class racer, proving that he is the most skilled teacher around—if not always the best tempered!

"NOW, LET'S **WORK THAT** VERTICAL."

Propeller perfectly waxed and polished

Skipper still wears the blue paint job from his Navy days.

Plane pals
Skipper's flying expertise and old war stories helped Dusty to become a champion, but Skipper also learned from Dusty to never give up. Now they are lifelong friends!

Happy ending
For many years Skipper refused to fly and was a grouchy loner, hardly venturing out of his hangar. After training Dusty, he is much happier and is even flying again!

Don't fly high

Traditional Leadbottom doesn't have time for dreamers like Dusty. He thinks having big ambitions is a waste of time—unless you're investing in a certain fertilizer!

Job offer
Old grouch Leadbottom cannot understand why Dusty ended a steady crop-dusting career to become a global racing legend adored by millions. He even offers Dusty his old job back!

Double wings are old-fashioned—but he doesn't care!

Vita-minamulch ad painted on his side

"I'M THE COMPOST KING!"

Leadbottom

Grumpy biplane Leadbottom runs a crop-spraying empire in Propwash Junction and was Dusty's old boss. The small town businessplane is obsessed with two things: making money and making vile-smelling Vita-minamulch. He loves the foul fertilizer's odor!

Gearbox Failure

A routine training flight ends in disaster when Dusty's gearbox fails and Skipper has to guide him in to land. Dottie cannot repair the gearbox and the factory no longer produces them. Unable to fly at full speed, Dusty may never race again! A new race begins to find a replacement gearbox.

Confident Dusty is not prepared for things to go wrong.

FUN FACT

When Dusty's gearbox fails he spins and falls out of the sky, but manages to regain control before hitting the water!

Dottie's diagnosis
Dottie examines Dusty and takes samples to find out what is wrong with him. She can tell Dusty's gearbox has begun to break down because she finds metal shavings from it inside his engine oil.

Speed dial

Flying too fast with the broken gearbox could cause Dusty to crash. Dottie fits a torque gauge so he can gauge his speed. If the needle goes into the red a warning light comes on. Then Dusty knows he must slow down before his engine seizes up!

TORQUE

30 40

20 50

10 60

FT/LB

7

X100

Accident takes place high over a winding river

"BUT DOTTIE. . . YOU'RE SAYING I CAN'T RACE ANYMORE!"

Skipper follows close behind Dusty on training flights.

1 Night flight
Dusty cannot believe he might never race again. In denial, he makes a lone night flight to prove he can still fly as fast as ever.

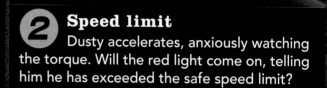

2 Speed limit
Dusty accelerates, anxiously watching the torque. Will the red light come on, telling him he has exceeded the safe speed limit?

DISASTER!

When Dusty accidentally smashes into Chug and Dottie's Fill 'n' Fly gas station, he causes a spectacular explosion! Soon a fierce fire is blazing, and it could spread. But aging fire truck Mayday with his worn-out equipment is completely unable to put out the flames.

③ Warning light!

The red warning light comes on! Dusty slows right down and is out of danger, but he has not been watching where he is going.

④ Smash 'n' crash

In a panic Dusty clips a tower and makes an emergency landing. Out of control, he crashes into the Fill 'n' Fly, which explodes!

⑤ Toppled tower

Dusty, Chug, and Skipper rush to help Mayday. The friends pull over the water tower, which crashes down, putting out the fire but causing even more damage to the town.

Mayday

Rescue truck Mayday is Propwash Junction's very own one-vehicle fire and rescue department. With decades of brave service behind him, aging Mayday is in desperate need of new equipment and a serious makeover. Corrosion and rust mean he is quite literally falling apart.

Rickety rescue

With his aching gears and his hose full of holes, Mayday is not as good at putting out fires as he once was. He may even get to the scene late, especially if he's had to return to the Fire Station to get his glasses. It's lucky fires are rare in sleepy Propwash Junction!

A helping wing

Mayday is worried that he will have to retire, but Dusty is determined to help his friend. He offers to train to be the town's second rescue vehicle!

"I'M GONNA NEED SOME HELP!"

Slightly dimmed light

Glittering career
In his Fire Station, Mayday keeps mementos and medals from his years of service. He has always been a dedicated and courageous firefighter.

Needs very powerful glasses

Modern Mayday
Dottie has worked out how to refurbish Mayday but it's no quick fix. He needs a new siren, roof turret, and foam cell—and that's just for starters!

TRUE OR FALSE?
Mayday has had contact lenses fitted to help him see better.

FALSE! He wears glasses, and he often forgets where he left them!

MAYDAY'S TOP 3 REFURBISHMENT WISH LIST

- Repairing the holes in his hose
- Fixing his corroded bumper before it falls off again
- A chain for his glasses so he doesn't forget or lose them

RYKER'S REPORT

After the fire at the Fill 'n' Fly, officers from the TMST (Transport Management Safety Team) arrive to investigate what went wrong. Inspector Ryker has the power to shut down any rescue service that is not up to scratch. He insists all rules are strictly followed, so Dusty and his friends know that Mayday is at risk of an epic fail!

Everyone waits for Ryker's verdict. If the rescue service is shut down, the airport must close too. There will be no visitors—and no Corn Festival!

TRUE OR FALSE?

TMST stands for This Means Serious Trouble.

FALSE! It stands for Transport Management Safety Team.

Skipper has a bad feeling about this.

Sparky holds his breath.

Dottie tries to look confident.

Firefighter Mayday was questioned in great detail about the incident at Propwash Junction.

TMST

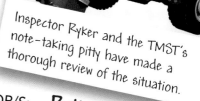

Inspector Ryker and the TMST's note-taking pitty have made a thorough review of the situation.

LOCATION: _Propwash Junction_

FIREFIGHTER/S: _Mayday_

INSPECTOR/S: _Ryker_

		PASS	FAIL
DID THE FIREFIGHTER RESPOND WITHIN 3 MINUTES? No. Firefighter had to return to Fire Station for his glasses.			✔
IS THE EQUIPMENT ADEQUATELY MAINTAINED? No. Hose full of holes, leaking nozzle, fire bell not securely fastened etc.			✔
ARE UP-TO-DATE SELF INSPECTION RECORDS AVAILABLE? No. Firefighter indicated that they did not keep records because there were no fires!			✔
IS A SECOND FIREFIGHTING VEHICLE PROVIDED? No. The sole firefighter asked locals to help put out the fire.			✔
ARE EMERGENCY PRODECURE PLANS IN PLACE? No. Evidence of toppled water tower suggests procedures are made up as they go along.			✔
IS THE FIREFIGHTER FIT FOR THE JOB? No. Firefighter has good service record but is out of date and out of breath.			

FAIL

WELCOME TO PISTON

Piston Peak is one America's most beautiful National Parks. Each year thousands of vehicles explore its spectacular cliffs, pristine forest, and crystal clear waters. Breathtaking views like these make Piston Peak picture-postcard perfect!

V-6 VALLEY

For many visitors, the V-6 Valley is the heart of the National Park. Traveling through the valley past the world-famous Piston Peak has revved the engines and fired the imagination of millions.

PISTON PEAK RAILROAD

The old Piston Peak Railroad winds through the Park, ending up at Fusel Lodge. This is one of America's most beautiful railway journeys. Passengers are on track for a fantastic ride.

FUSEL LODGE

Fusel Lodge is the ultimate luxury hotel. No expense has been spared in making this *the* place to stay for discerning visitors to Piston Peak National Park. In fact, guests stay in such incredible comfort they may feel tempted not to leave the hotel!

WHITEWALL FALLS

Whitewall Falls, in Augerin Canyon, is an unforgettable sight. The majestic bridge, backed by the waterfall cascading down a sheer cliff, is one of the park's most magical spots.

AUGERIN CANYON

Augerin Canyon is a deep ravine with a wild, twisting river at the bottom. Its rocky arches and strange stone formations offer guests some exciting flying opportunities.

GASKET GEYSER

Located in front of Fusel Lodge, Gasket Geyser regularly shoots massive jets of boiling water and steam high into the air. It's a spectacular sight. This is one gasket that you will want to see blow!

PISTON PEAK AIR ATTACK BASE

In Piston Peak National Park the air attack base is the central HQ for fire and rescue operations. After agreeing to train as a firefighter, nervous Dusty is sent here to join a group of the most plucky planes, heroic helicopters, and valiant vehicles around. When a wildfire burns out of control, these guys are hot stuff at putting it out!

Windlifter's hangar

Blade's hangar

Lil' Dipper's hangar

Dusty's hangar

Cabbie's hangar

The air attack base looks like nothing fancy. Corrugated steel hangars nestle together, close to a small runway.

Meet the team

If he is to learn quickly and get certified as a firefighter, Dusty must get to know the rescue crew as soon as possible. Luckily Dusty is not too shy and the team is (mostly) friendly.

Ground crew

Not only planes and helicopters make up the rescue team. The smokejumpers are a team of trusty trucks who work on the ground, bravely clearing forest areas in the path of the fire.

Radio home

Alone in his new hangar, Dusty gets a little homesick. Thankfully there is a radio so he can talk to Chug, Dottie, and Skipper back in Propwash Junction. They always lift his spirits!

Blade Ranger

Courageous copter Blade Ranger heads up the air attack base at Piston Peak. The rescue chief is a tough taskmaster, but he is incredibly loyal and has the respect of all his team. Blade may seem serious, but that's because he is seriously dedicated to saving lives!

TRUE OR FALSE?

Blade starred in the '80s cop TV show *Propeller Patrol*.

FALSE! It was '70s show CHoPs.

Copter coach

New recruit Dusty learns that he must undergo intensive one-to-one training with Blade. Blade proves to be a demanding teacher, but he is extra patient with newbie Dusty, who can sometimes be overconfident!

Rule maker

Blade expects the attack team to follow his rules, and he rarely relaxes them. Like the rest of the team, Dusty must understand that safety comes first!

TV tough guy

Blade used to be a megastar in '70s television show *CHoPS*, about a pair of rescue helicopters. But something happened that made him turn his back on TV and become a real rescue helicopter. Now Blade never mentions the time when he was famous.

Tail propeller to help maintain low hovering

Always concentrates and remains focused

Blade's powerful blades

301

Hoist hero

Nobody is more skillful at using a rescue hoist than Blade. Lifting a wildlife-tractor away to safety from a raging wildfire is all in a day's work for him!

"WHEN I TELL YOU TO DO SOMETHING, YOU DO IT!"

"CHOPS"

It's the coolest buddy cop show ever to hit your TV screen! Ride with Blade and Nick of the California Helicopter Patrol for thrills, spills, and the smoothest stunt skills ever.

Keeping the BAD GUYS out of the SKIES!

"Bloozin'" Blade Ranger

This dude is seriously cool! Get from "Bloozin'" Blade of flip you'll is a backflip with a sideslip and is a rotor-rattling roll!

Nick "Loop 'n' " Lopez

Nick "Loop 'n' " Lopez and an head for heights and an head for heights and an head for your motors "Loop 'n' " Lopez will get your motors turnin' for sure! He's the smooth-talking hero with a head for the ladies. "Loop 'n' " Lopez burnin' and rotors turnin' for sure! eye for the ladies.

Sky-high tension and smokin' hot adventures!

Fun, laughs, and best buddy action!

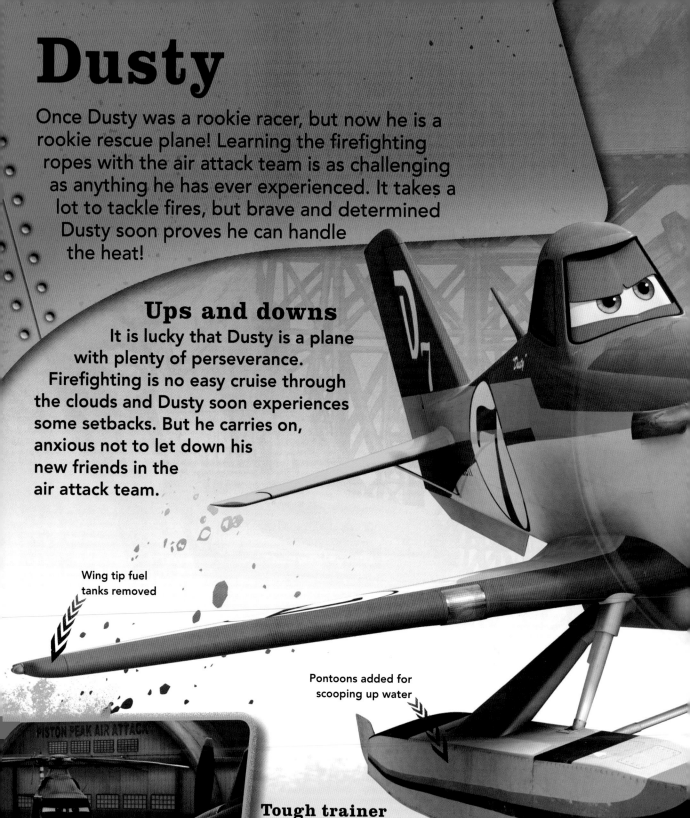

Dusty

Once Dusty was a rookie racer, but now he is a rookie rescue plane! Learning the firefighting ropes with the air attack team is as challenging as anything he has ever experienced. It takes a lot to tackle fires, but brave and determined Dusty soon proves he can handle the heat!

Ups and downs

It is lucky that Dusty is a plane with plenty of perseverance. Firefighting is no easy cruise through the clouds and Dusty soon experiences some setbacks. But he carries on, anxious not to let down his new friends in the air attack team.

Wing tip fuel tanks removed

Pontoons added for scooping up water

Tough trainer

Veteran helicopter Blade is responsible for transforming Dusty from trainee to fully-fledged fire plane. It is a big ask! To start with Blade is not impressed by Dusty's efforts.

Maru's modifications

Engineering genius Maru retrofits Dusty for his new role. Maru removes Dusty's fuel tanks and landing gear, and welds on two water pontoons.

DUSTY'S TOP 3
PISTON PEAK MOMENTS

- Getting praise from Blade
- Finding out he is braver than he ever thought
- Making a new set of lifelong friends

"THIS IS TOUGHER THAN I THOUGHT!"

TRUE OR FALSE?

At the air attack base, Dusty has his landing gear completely removed.

TRUE! It's one of the modifications made by Maru.

Fitting in

Dusty may be a champ racer, but he does not get any star treatment! He has to work hard before he is allowed to fly alongside the team.

DUSTY'S TRAINING ROUTINE

Becoming a rescue plane takes skill, courage, and plenty of practice! For Dusty to become a firefighter he must undergo an ultra-tough training regime devised by Blade Ranger. Training on Piston Peak's treacherous terrain tests and stretches Dusty to his very limits!

1 Maneuvering

The park is full of twisting canyons and tight rocky ravines that need to be maneuvered through. Flying too high near the rim, too low over the river, or too close to the cliffs could result in a crash!

2 Pulling up

Fighting flames sometimes means flying as close to the fire as possible, before making a sudden escape. Flying under the bridge and then pulling up sharply before Dusty hits the canyon cliff is perfect practice.

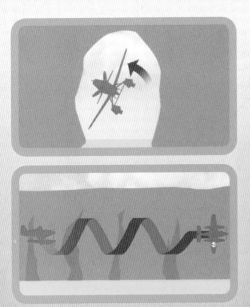

③ Banking and rolling

The rocks in the park form tricky arches that are so narrow that planes must fly on their sides to get through them. Banking to one side and mastering a corkscrew roll is critical to learn the flying control required—even if it does leave Dusty in a spin!

④ Scooping water

Dusty's new pontoons can scoop water from the lake and drop it onto a fire, but it is not easy! Dusty needs a 50-foot approach, 15 seconds skimming the lake, and a sharp climb in order to clear the trees.

⑤ Target practice

Pinpoint accuracy in dropping fire retardant is essential! Burning barrels make great practice targets. Unfortunately Dusty's crop-spraying experience does not count for much—at first, his aim is terrible!

Maru

Ace mechanic Maru must be the most gifted forklift in Piston Peak. He combines creativity with engineering ingenuity to recycle spare parts and rebuild bits of machinery so they are better than new. Without Maru's repairs, the cash-strapped air attack base would fall apart!

MARU'S TOP 3 FEATS OF ENGINEERING

🔥 Building Patch's control tower

🔥 Fixing Blade up after he is seriously injured

🔥 Dusty's custom-made epicyclic concentric reduction gearbox

Master engineer

Maru is proud of his engineering skills. His world-class welding and talent with tools make him a master craftsman in his hangar.

"THEY'RE BETTER THAN NEW."

Spare parts

Maru's workshop shelves are full of junk. But is it really junk? Any one of these spare parts could one day be recycled for a truly essential repair.

Wall of Fame

A "Wall of Fame" in Maru's workshop shows photos of every air attack plane who has crashed. Dusty is a bit worried when Maru takes his picture for it!

TRUE OR FALSE?

Maru is afraid of water and avoids any jobs that involve using it.

FALSE! One of his regular duties is power-washing.

Multi-tasking Maru

Repairing, towing equipment, welding, power-washing, helping Blade to train, and operating the radio are just some of Maru's many jobs on base. As well as working hard, the funny forklift keeps up a stream of witty one-liners!

Extra grip on tires helps shift heavy loads

Versatile forklifts for welding and lifting

Lil' Dipper

Cheerful, bubbly Lil' Dipper puts out fires by picking up water from a lake and then dropping it to drown the flames. Lil' Dipper's liveliness may be a bit full-on, but this super-scooper is far from dippy! In fact she's one of the most focused firefighters around!

Drop and drench

In one hour, Lil' Dipper can drench a fire with more gallons of water than anyone else. She's also a hotshot with the team's special red fire retardant.

Twin propellers for speedy getaways

"AW...THAT IS SO SWEET."

Passionate plane

Lil' Dipper loves being a rescue plane and always gives 101 percent effort! She used to be stuck in a boring job transporting goods over the icy tundra of Alaska, but found fighting fires lifted her spirits more than lifting cargo ever could!

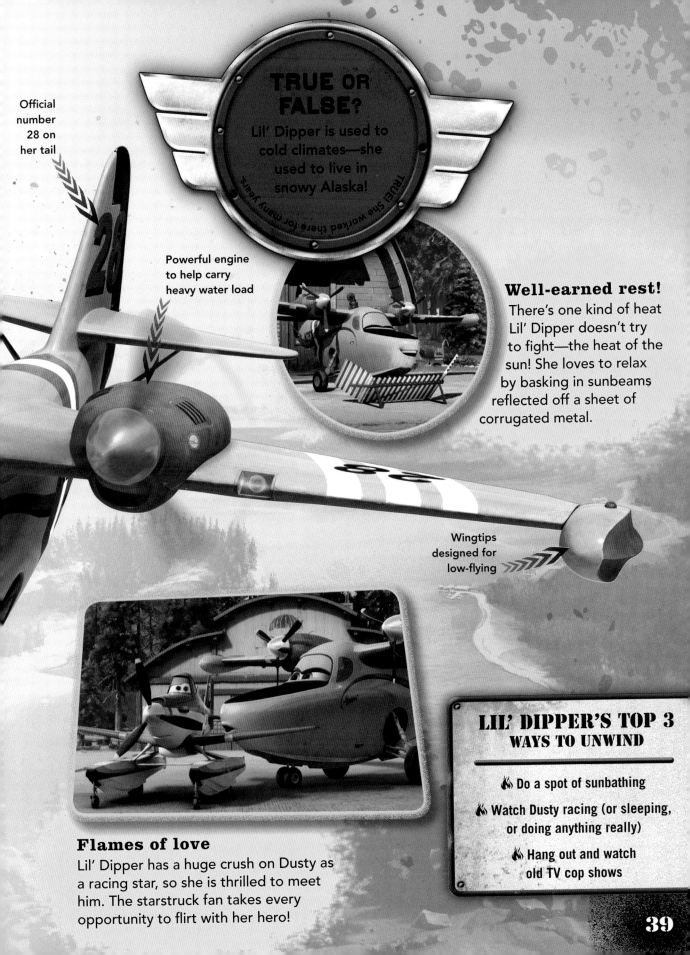

Official number 28 on her tail

TRUE OR FALSE?

Lil' Dipper is used to cold climates—she used to live in snowy Alaska!

TRUE! She worked there for many years.

Powerful engine to help carry heavy water load

Well-earned rest!

There's one kind of heat Lil' Dipper doesn't try to fight—the heat of the sun! She loves to relax by basking in sunbeams reflected off a sheet of corrugated metal.

Wingtips designed for low-flying

Flames of love

Lil' Dipper has a huge crush on Dusty as a racing star, so she is thrilled to meet him. The starstruck fan takes every opportunity to flirt with her hero!

LIL' DIPPER'S TOP 3
WAYS TO UNWIND

- 🔥 Do a spot of sunbathing
- 🔥 Watch Dusty racing (or sleeping, or doing anything really)
- 🔥 Hang out and watch old TV cop shows

39

Windlifter

Huge helicopter Windlifter is the guy to call on when things get heavy! He can carry massive loads of fire retardant, and his strength during rescues is legendary. The quiet Native American also has a wry sense of humor, telling old folklore tales with unexpected endings!

"WE NEED EVERY PLANE WE'VE GOT."

Base buddies
Windlifter's best pal on base is Lil' Dipper. Loud, lively Lil' Dipper and quiet Windlifter could not be more different, but they have lots of fun together!

Strong and high wheels for lift-off and landing

WINDLIFTER'S TOP 3 FAVORITE TALES

🔥 The legend of Haoka, who beats his drums to make thunder

🔥 An ancient toast about Coyote, who ate his own tires to renew himself

🔥 Anything that will mystify a newbie!

Blade boost
Windlifter's powerful rotor gives him the edge when lifting loads. However, it is his bravery that gives him the biggest boost of all.

Windlifter's wisdom

From his Native American background Windlifter has acquired a deep knowledge of forest folklore, and can sense danger from fire just by listening and feeling the wind. His instincts are always right—it is not just hot air!

TRUE OR FALSE?

Before he was a fire rescue plane, Windlifter was a lumberjack.

TRUE! But in the end he got bored of chopping trees.

Huge, powerful rotor

Windlifter is a serious-looking dude

Log lifter

Windlifter has many strengths, but the best of them is his sheer power. The former lumberjack likes to keep fit by hoisting tons of heavy trees.

Cabbie

Ex-army aircraft Cabbie is a key member of the air attack team. A cool, calm cargo plane, he carries the smokejumpers to the scene of a fire and makes sure they land safely. Cabbie's military mind helps him to stay focused, even when he is joking around with the smokejumpers!

CABBIE'S TOP 3 MISSION SAFETY TIPS

🔥 Find a safe spot for the smokejumpers to land before giving the green light

🔥 Get confirmation of a safe landing

🔥 Always maintain radio contact

Ramp it up!

You never know when a fire will start, so Cabbie has to be ready to roll at a moment's notice. When it is time, he lowers his ramp for the smokejumpers to get on board!

TRUE OR FALSE?

Cabbie's nickname for the smokejumpers is the mud munchers.

FALSE! It's the gravel crunchers!

Buddy banter

Cabbie enjoys bantering with the smokejumpers. He calls them gravel crunchers because their tires can cope with the roughest terrain.

Radio antennas

Firmly secured back ramp

On the radio

During missions, Cabbie spends long periods of time on the radio. In his spare time, he spends long periods of time listening to the radio... ham radio!

Powerful twin engines for longer haul flights

"WE GOT THAT SUCKER BOXED IN!"

Old soldier

Cabbie used to be in the military, carrying a cargo of jeeps to parachute down behind enemy lines. Once he retired he missed the action. He soon got refitted so he could use his skill and years of experience to help put fires out.

43

Patch

Patch is the air attack team's air traffic controller. Working in her tall control tower, she sounds the alarm, sends the aircraft out, and monitors their position. Eagle-eyed Patch never misses a fire starting in the park. If something is going on in her patch, Patch knows about it!

Patch's brain is always processing the latest data.

Calm and clear

Being well-organized and reliable are important in Patch's job. She always makes her instructions crystal clear as they are broadcast over the loud speaker or through the radio. She is also the tidiest tug on base, cleaning the windows of her tower every day.

Control tower

Patch's control tower was built by Maru from recycled materials. The tower creaks whenever it is windy, but Patch has gotten used to that now.

Patch can pitch in with loading if needed.

Ready to rock!

When the base is scrambling for a rescue mission, Patch plays loud rock music on her record player. It helps to get everybody pumped up!

PATCH'S TOP 3
HIGH-RISK SITUATIONS

🔥 Multiple fires needing attention at the same time

🔥 High winds fanning the flames

🔥 Thick smoke causing poor visibility for flying

"LISTEN UP Y'ALL... WE GOT BIG TROUBLE."

Always looks smart, neat, and tidy

TRUE OR FALSE?

Patch plays soothing music to calm everyone's nerves before a big emergency.

FALSE: She plays heavy rock music to raise the energy levels!

Well equipped

The control tower has all the equipment that resourceful Patch needs to monitor dangerous situations. Maps on her screen show fires blazing and planes flying while constant radio contact keeps her up-to-date.

Smokejumpers

The smokejumpers must be the bravest clear-up crew around! These five all-terrain vehicles parachute out of Cabbie and into danger, landing close to wildfires and clearing the ground to prevent flames spreading. Working as a team, they use their tools to chop, drop, lift, and shift trees and logs.

Dynamite

Dynamic Dynamite co-ordinates the action on the ground and reports back to the rescue planes via radio.

Drip

Drip has plenty of grip! His powerful mechanical grabber moves chopped trees with ease.

Pinecone

Pinecone puts a fine comb to the forest floor, gathering and raking away brush before it can ignite.

Blackout

With his razor-sharp saw, Blackout is a whiz at sawing through trees. This brave ATV has logged many missions!

Avalanche

Avalanche is a mini-bulldozer whose job is moving tree debris. When push comes to shove, you can rely on him!

Riding the Silk Elevator

1

Get ready!

A report of a fire has come in! The fearless five click on their parachute packs and roll backward into Cabbie, ready for take-off.

2

Jump!

When the green light goes on, it's time to leap! The smokejumpers deploy their parachutes, landing in a safe clearing close to the fire.

3

Clear!

The smokejumpers get to work immediately, working together quickly to chop trees, sweep brush, and clear debris until the area is safe.

GO, TEAM, GO!

Electrical storms are a serious threat in Piston Peak National Park. Lightning strikes can cause multiple wildfires to break out simultaneously! When Patch spots these blazes she gives Blade their locations. He quickly assesses the situation—then gets the gang into gear and sends the planes out to where they can make their special skills count.

AIR ATTACK BASE

THUNDERBOLT BLUFFS

6

1 Lil' Dipper

Lil' Dipper is sent to Anchor Lake. Her mission is to scoop water and drop it on a fire near Rail Ridge to the east.

PARK ENTRANCE

4

FUSEL LODGE

5

LA PARRILLA

2 Windlifter

Windlifter flies out to lofty Canopy Dome. There, he will sense which way the fire will go and drop retardant on its outer edge.

V-6 VALLEY

Blade

Blade heads for Augerin Canyon. He will maneuver between a wall of flames and a rockface to hoist a stranded vehicle to safety.

Cabbie

Cabbie flies steadily west over Fusel Lodge. He will look for the safest spot to drop the smokejumpers in blazing V-6 Valley.

CANOPY DOME

WHITEWALL FALLS

RAIL RIDGE

ANCHOR LAKE

AUGERIN CANYON

PISTON PEAK

Smokejumpers

The smokejumpers parachute into a forested part of V-6 valley. They clear the area in the fire's path, stopping it from spreading.

Dusty

Blade will not send Dusty out alone before he is fully trained. But with so many fires burning, all wings are needed in the air! Blade escorts Dusty to a small fire below Thunderbolt Bluffs, and keeps an eye on his trainee as he successfuly drops his retardant.

N
W   E
S

Fusel Lodge

The magnificent five-story Fusel Lodge has been welcoming guests to Piston Peak National Park for years. Now the rustic-style lodge has been refurbished as the ultimate luxury hotel, boasting a stylish bar, a sumptuous spa, and a huge honeymoon suite. There is even a zero-emission, eco-friendly floor!

Every balcony has a personal helipad.

Reopening night

Cad Spinner makes sure Fusel Lodge's grand reopening party is a night to remember. The sleek hotel twinkles with lights, and the chatter of excited guests floats on the breeze while laser beams sweep back and forth across the night sky. It is an impressive sight!

On the list

Cad has invited all the hottest stars of stage, screen, and stadium to the glittering opening party. Flashbulbs pop as the celebrities make their entrance, while excited guests wait behind the velvet rope, hoping for a glimpse of their favorite.

Checking in

The first hotel guests check in to their rooms. A pair of young newlyweds will be the first to enjoy the deluxe honeymoon suite with its romantic view of Piston Peak.

Chilling out

After rubbing shoulders with the stars and sampling Fusel Lodge's fine facilites, guests can relax and chill out. A staff pitty is on hand to bring them anything they desire.

Control tower designed as an architectural feature

Return visitors

Harvey and Winnie were honeymooners at Piston Peak 50 years ago. The elderly RVs are even more in love now, and are back to look for the spot where they first kissed.

The Lodge's famous veranda

"WHOA...LOOK AT THIS PLACE!"

Cad Spinner

Cad Spinner may be the Piston Peak National Park Superintendent, but he is far from super. In fact this SUV is a Selfish Unpleasant Vehicle! Cad only cares about one thing—himself! Unfortunately Cad is the park boss and the manager of Fusel Lodge, so he can order everyone about!

TRUE OR FALSE?

Cad does not know who Dusty is and does not invite him to the Fusel Lodge opening party.

FALSE! Cad would love to have global superstars there.

Rude dude

Unkind Cad insults everybody around him so that he can feel superior and get his way. The loudmouthed lout has no respect for anybody, unless they are famous!

Safety last

Cad has cut most of the budget for Piston Peak's fire and rescue department so that he has more to spend on his luxury hotel, Fusel Lodge. Impressing guests means more to him than keeping them safe. He even puts their lives at risk by refusing to evacuate the park when fire threatens.

"SUPERINTENDENT COMING. I SIGN YOUR PAYCHECKS!"

Famous faces

Shallow Cad only wants to mix with star cars and VIPs—Very Important Planes! He has even invited a top politician, the Secretary of the Interior, to the Lodge's launch party!

Luxury Lodge

Cad thinks the remodel of Fusel Lodge will make him rich and important. He does not want anything to spoil it. Trucks must wipe their muddy tires before entering!

CAD'S TOP 3
ESSENTIAL ITEMS FOR THE LODGE LAUNCH PARTY

- Famous or important guests like Dusty Crophopper and the Secretary of the Interior
- An arty ice sculpture, made to impress
- Lots of expensive food, luxury drinks, and over-helpful staff

Untrustworthy eyes

Loud mouth always giving out insults

Piston Peak National Park emblem

Park Staff

The staff at Piston Peak work hard to help guests enjoy the facilities. Sadly, they are way too busy working for their obnoxious boss, Cad Spinner, to enjoy anything themselves! As Fusel Lodge's grand reopening draws near, Cad is putting them under more pressure than ever.

Nozzle pumps out water to put out flames >>>>>

Pulaski

Fire engine Pulaski is a proud member of the Piston Peak Fire Department, and works hard to keep Fusel Lodge flame free. Safety conscious Pulaski always stays calm under pressure—and you need to be calm if you work for Cad!

Regulation >>>> issue fire safety helmet

Rake

Rake is a fire pitty who partners up with Pulaski. No-nonsense Rake just wants to get the job done, and can be pretty fiery himself when he is at work. If Rake has his fire shield down, do not get in his way!

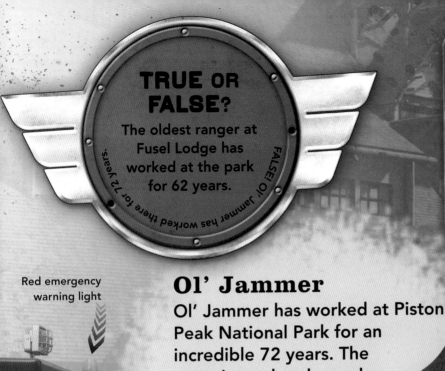

Red emergency warning light

Ol' Jammer

Ol' Jammer has worked at Piston Peak National Park for an incredible 72 years. The experienced and popular ranger knows everything about the park's wildlife, as well as how to manage wild crowds of visitors!

Jammer feels honored to wear the Park emblem.

Permanently nervous expression

André the Concierge Pitty

André greets guests at Fusel Lodge, carries their bags, and tends to their needs. Ever anxious to please, he often ends up just anxious—mainly from being pulled in different directions by guests' requests and Cad's orders.

Park Fire!

When a lightning storm strikes in the park, it often starts many small fires. In dry forest conditions, these could easily merge into one huge, raging inferno. A fire this size must be dealt with swiftly or it could rip through the park, endangering the lives of visitors. Quick—call the air attack team!

Rail Ridge, a popular spot in the National Park

"THIS IS A *BIG ONE!*"

Ready for Action

The air attack team is on permanent alert. These perfect professionals have practiced the drill so many times that they can be kitted out and fired up to fight the flames in minutes.

Thick smoke severely limits flying visibility.

The rescue team must get close to dangerous flames.

FUN FACT

All the team members used to have other jobs but really found their wings fighting fires.

1 Piston Peak burning

As the fire rages through the park, the flames begin to surround the hotel. The wooden lodge is in danger of catching alight!

2 Cutting corners

Cad would rather save Fusel Lodge than save the guests! He diverts air attack's life-saving water supply to the hotel sprinklers.

FUSEL LODGE RESCUE

A raging fire sweeps toward Fusel Lodge, but Cad Spinner refuses to evacuate. Overconfident as ever, he tells himself it is only a small fire and will soon blow over. With Blade Ranger down after receiving ~~serious~~ injuries shielding Dusty from the flames, it is left to Windlifter to take command.

3 Fusel Lodge sprinklers
The roof sprinklers erupt with water that could have been better used in making precious fire retardant for the air attack team.

4 Plucky Pulaski
Park staff rebel against Cad, and begin to evacuate the lodge and park. Heroic Pulaski leads the evacuation routine.

5 Evacuate!
At last the hotel is evacuated. Pulaski and his colleagues guide the guests calmly out to the runway or on to a waiting train. Meanwhile, without their leader and with limited fire retardant, the air attack team bravely battles the fire.

Dusty the Hero

Just when it seems that all guests are safe, the team gets some terrible news. Winnie and Harvey have become trapped by fire in the canyon while looking for the spot where they had their first kiss. Determined to make up for causing Blade's injuries, Dusty heads off solo, going against Blade's rules about night flying.

Thick smoke reduces visibility even more

FUN FACT

Dusty does half-loops, barrel rolls, and snap rolls in his bid to rescue Winnie and Harvey from the bridge.

"I CAN DO IT!"

Ultra-hot flames...feel the heat!

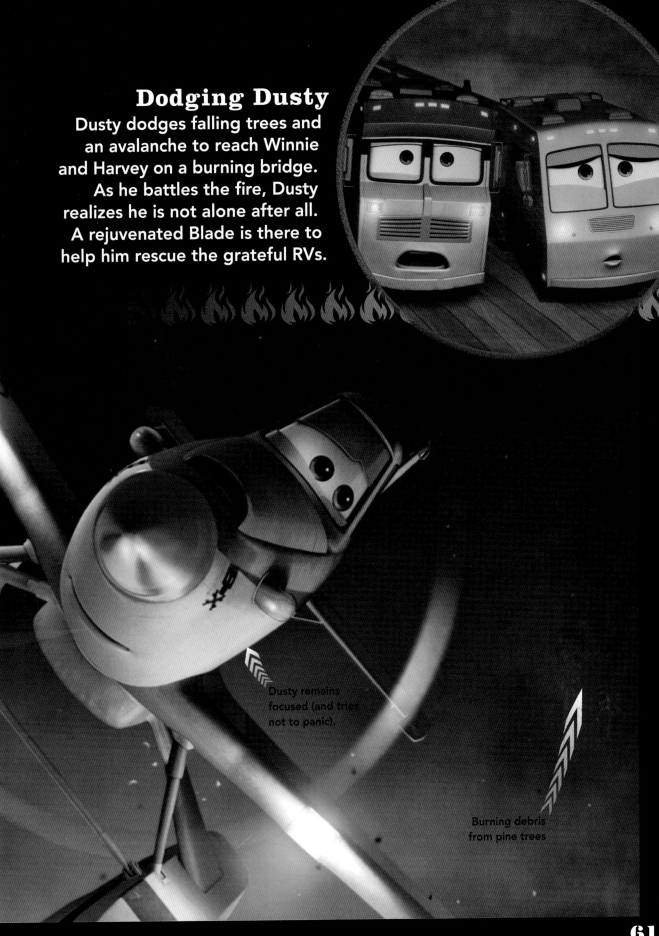

Dodging Dusty

Dusty dodges falling trees and an avalanche to reach Winnie and Harvey on a burning bridge. As he battles the fire, Dusty realizes he is not alone after all. A rejuvenated Blade is there to help him rescue the grateful RVs.

Dusty remains focused (and tries not to panic).

Burning debris from pine trees

Propwash Junction Corn Fest

The annual Corn Festival is the event of the year in Propwash Junction. It has even made the national news! Visitors always love coming to the Corn Fest celebrations, however, this year is extra special. The festival features an amazing aerial demonstration from the town's new firefighter Dusty (with a custom made gearbox courtesy of clever Maru) and special guests the Piston Peak Air Attack Team!

Propwash Junction is surrounded by beautiful countryside.

Brand new paint job

Stunt ramps with the smokejumpers' emblem

Spectacular smokejumpers

The smokejumpers carry out breathtaking stunts to wow the crowds! They ride fast to the top of the ramp and then leap high in the air, doing acrobatic flips. Their firefighting has made them fearless and their skill means these guys truly defy gravity!

Sky's the limit

Dusty and the air attack team give a fabulous flying display full of dangerous diving, rolling, climbing, and dropping water, all at incredible speed. The crowd is gripped with excitement. They roar as they watch the sky! Dusty's pals are so proud of their buddy.

RV rest and relaxation

Retired RVs Winnie and Harvey need another holiday to recover after Dusty rescued them from the fire at Piston Peak! Attending the Corn Fest is the perfect way to relax and catch up with all their new friends from the air attack team.

ACKNOWLEDGMENTS

DK

LONDON, NEW YORK,
MELBOURNE, MUNICH, AND DELHI

Senior Designer Lisa Robb
Design by Lisa Robb, Toby Truphet
Editor Julia March
Editorial Assistant Lauren Nesworthy
Pre-Production Producer Marc Staples
Senior Producer Alex Bell
Managing Editor Laura Gilbert
Managing Art Editor Maxine Pedliham
Art Director Lisa Lanzarini
Publishing Manager Julie Ferris
Publishing Director Simon Beecroft

First Published in the United States in 2014
by DK Publishing, 345 Hudson Street,
New York, New York 10014

10 9 8 7 6 5 4 3
007–196544–June/14

Published in Great Britain by Dorling Kindersley Limited

DK books are available at special discounts when purchased in bulk
for sales promotions, premiums, fund-raising, or educational use.
For details, contact: DK Publishing Special Markets,
345 Hudson Street, New York, New York 10014
Special Sales@dk.com

A CIP catalog record for this book
is available from the Library of Congress

ISBN 978-1-4654-2022-0

Color reproduction by Alta Image, UK
Printed and bound in China by Hung Hing

DK would like to thank Chelsea Alon,
Heather Knowles, Tony Fejeran, Caroline Egan, Ryan Ferguson,
and John-Paul Orpinas at Disney Publishing,
and Paul Gerard from DisneyToon Studios.